The Hare
the Tortoise

Retold by Jenny Giles
Illustrated by Pat Reynolds

NELSON PRICE MILBURN

Once upon a time,
some animals lived near a big meadow.
Every day, they would meet together,
and Hare would come jumping along
to join them.

Hare would dance and prance
through the long grass, telling them all
what a fine fellow he was.
"I am the best runner in the land,"
he would boast.
"No one could win a race against me."

The animals always turned away
from Hare and took no notice of him.

But one hot afternoon,
Tortoise came crawling slowly out
from behind his rock.
"I am tired of listening to your boasting,"
said Tortoise,
"so I will give you a race, Hare."

"You!" laughed Hare.
"Why, you are the slowest animal in the land.
What sort of race would that be?"

"A race like any other race," said Tortoise,
"and it can take place whenever you like."

The animals all cheered,
and their noise awoke the wise old Owl.
"If Tortoise wants to race Hare,
then he shall," hooted Owl.
"I will start the race myself."

"You will go once around the track
by the meadow," he said,
"past the willow tree,
and back to this tree."
Hare jumped out onto the track
and stood there waiting.
The little mice scratched a starting line
from the tree to the rock
with their tiny paws.

Tortoise crawled slowly down to the line.

"Take your marks!
Get set! Hoo-oo-oot!" called Owl.

Hare got away to a fine start,
and he was soon out of sight.
"Why am I having a race
with the slowest animal in the land?"
he asked himself.
"I am just wasting my time."

Tortoise moved his legs
slowly up and down as he plodded along.
"The sun is very hot," he said to himself,
"but my shell is keeping me cool.
I will be able to walk
all around the meadow today."

Soon Hare stopped and looked behind him.
He couldn't see Tortoise anywhere.
"I've got time to have a little rest,"
he said.
"Tortoise won't be here for hours."

So Hare sat down to rest
in the shade of the willow tree.
He lay back in the cool green grass
and watched the leaves moving gently
above him.
His eyes began to close
and his head began to nod.
Very soon, Hare was asleep.

Meanwhile, Tortoise,
who had been plodding steadily along,
could just see the willow tree
in the distance.

The little mice came running up to him.
"Good news, Tortoise," they squeaked.
"Hare has gone to sleep!"

Tortoise smiled to himself
and crawled just a little bit faster.

At last, he reached the willow tree. Very quietly, he crept past Hare and headed towards the finish line.

All the animals watched as Tortoise plodded on, getting closer and closer to the finish line. They began to shout, "Come on, Tortoise!" "You're nearly there!" "You're going to win!"

All the shouting and cheering
woke Hare up.
He couldn't believe his eyes
when he saw Tortoise ahead of him!
"I still have time to win," he cried,
and he set off as fast as he could go.

"Look out, Tortoise! Hare is coming!"
called the animals.

Owl looked down, and he saw Tortoise put his foot over the finish line first.

Hare raced across, but he was too late.

"Tortoise wins!" hooted Owl.
All the animals cheered.

Hare felt very foolish,
and he crept away into the meadow.

"Ah, well," said Owl,
as he looked down at the animals.
"Slow and steady wins the race!"

A play
The Hare and the Tortoise

People in the play

Reader	 Squirrel
 Hare	 Duck
 Tortoise	 First Mouse
 Owl	 Second Mouse

Badger

Reader

Once upon a time,
some animals lived near a big meadow.
Every day, they would meet together,
and Hare would come jumping along
to join them.
Hare would dance and prance
through the long grass, telling them all
what a fine fellow he was.

Hare

I am the best runner in the land.
No one could win a race against me.

Badger

Oh, go away, Hare.

Squirrel

We know what a good runner you are.

Duck

And we don't want to race against you.

Reader

But one hot afternoon,
Tortoise came crawling slowly out
from behind his rock.

Tortoise

I am tired of listening to your boasting,
Hare, so I will give you a race.

Hare

You! Why, you are the slowest animal
in the land.
What sort of race would that be?

Tortoise

A race like any other race,
and it can take place whenever you like.

Badger

Hurrah for Tortoise!

Squirrel

You can do it!

Duck

Good for you, Tortoise!

Reader

All the noise awoke the wise old Owl,
who had been asleep in his tree
above the animals.

Owl

If Tortoise wants to race Hare,
then he shall.
I will start the race myself.
You will go once around the track
by the meadow, past the willow tree,
and back to this tree.

Hare

I am ready to start.

First Mouse

We will make a line from the tree
to the rock.

Second Mouse

The race can begin from here.

Reader

Everyone watched quietly as Tortoise crawled slowly down to the line.

Owl

Take your marks! Get set! Hoo-oo-oot!

Reader

Hare got away to a fine start, and he was soon out of sight.

Hare

Why am I having a race
with the slowest animal in the land?
I am just wasting my time.

Reader

Tortoise moved his legs
slowly up and down as he plodded along.

Tortoise

The sun is very hot,
but my shell is keeping me cool.
I will be able to walk
all around the meadow today.

Reader

Soon Hare stopped
and looked behind him.

Hare

I've got time to have a little rest
under this willow tree.
Tortoise won't be here for hours.

Reader

Hare lay back in the cool green grass
and watched the leaves moving gently
above him.
His eyes began to close
and his head began to nod.
Very soon, Hare was asleep.
Meanwhile, Tortoise had been plodding
steadily along.

Tortoise

I can see the willow tree
in the distance.
I will reach it in a little while.

Reader

The little mice came running
up to Tortoise.

First Mouse

We have some good news for you, Tortoise.

Second Mouse

Hare has gone to sleep
under the willow tree.

Reader

Tortoise smiled to himself
and crawled just a little bit faster.

Tortoise

Aah! I have reached the willow tree
and Hare is still asleep.
I will creep past him very quietly.

Reader

So Tortoise went past Hare
and headed towards the finish line.
The animals saw him coming,
and began to shout.

Badger

Look! Here comes Tortoise!

Squirrel

Come on, Tortoise! You're nearly there!

Duck

You're going to win!

Hare (waking up)

Oh, no! How did Tortoise get past me?
I will have to hurry to catch him,
but I still have time to win.

Badger
Look out, Tortoise!

Squirrel
Hare is awake!

Duck
Hare is coming!

Reader
Owl looked down, and he saw Tortoise put his foot over the finish line first. Hare raced across, but he was too late.

Owl
Tortoise wins!

Badger

Hurrah for Tortoise!

Squirrel

Tortoise got here first!

Duck

Tortoise has won the race!

Reader

Hare felt very foolish,
and he crept away
into the meadow.

Owl

Ah, well...
slow and steady wins the race!